Illustrations by Csongor Veres
www.csongorveres.tumblr.com

First Printing 2016

Printed in the United States of America

D1567289

Ellie & Elliot

A Story about Autism

Written by Chasiti Wachter

Illustrated by Csongor Veres

For Carson: my son and my inspiration.

Thank you for the light you bring into our lives and the joy of seeing the world through your eyes, and thank you to your siblings, your biggest supporters and your best friends, Maddy & Evan. May you only have happy days and know how very loved you are.

And a special thanks to the teachers, therapists and staff at Step By Step Academy and Nationwide Children's Hospital.

Lastly, I would like to thank you, the reader, for your support.

My name is Ellie.
I have a big brother named Elliot.

Elliot has Autism.
Autism is a brain disorder
that affects Elliot in many ways.

Elliot was born with Autism.
Autism is just one of the many things
that make Elliot who he is.

Elliot is just like you and me.
He loves to spray water from his trunk.

He loves to graze in the
sun, and he loves to play in the mud.

Elliot is different from you and me, too.
At first, I didn't understand
why Elliot didn't want to play with me.
Mommy said Elliot feels better playing by himself.

Autism makes it difficult for Elliot to be a part of the herd.
He isn't interested in other elephants.

I love when Elliot wraps his trunk around mine
and welcomes me into his world.
He loves when I chase him,
and I love to make him giggle.

Elliot communicates with Mommy and Daddy by squeezing their trunks when he wants a hug.

Elliot has sensory difficulties.
This means that he doesn't like bright lights,
loud noises, or certain smells.

Any of these things can make Elliot feel unhappy,
and we don't always know what to expect from him.

Elliot can do many things extraordinarily well,
but some of the things that are easy for us are harder for him,
like counting peanuts or playing water games.
Mommy says this is a part of Autism,
and Elliot has special teachers who help him with these skills.

Elliot is so smart, and he has taught me so much.
He has taught me to appreciate the little things,
like a bird flying in the sky, or the perfect edges of a rock.
He has taught me how to be compassionate
since he needs a little extra help sometimes.

I look forward to learning new things from Elliot,
and to teaching him new things, too.

The next time you see an elephant playing alone,
or who may be having a hard time,
think about Elliot, and try to remember
that elephant might have Autism, too.

Chasiti Wachter is a mother of three. Her oldest was diagnosed with autism when he was two and she has been dedicated to the cause since then. She is an advocate for the autism community and she believes that advocacy can make a difference in the lives of these individuals and their families. Chasiti likes to emphasize the importance of early intervention and treatments. She resides in Columbus, Ohio with her husband and their three children.

35291013R00019

Made in the USA
Lexington, KY
02 April 2019